HITLER'S WAR MACHINE

THE WAFFEN SS IN THE WEST

A REPRINT OF THE 1941
GERMAN PHOTOGRAPHIC JOURNAL

WITH ENGLISH CAPTIONS AND ANNOTATIONS.

Introduced and Edited by Bob Carruthers

Pen & Sword
MILITARY

This edition published in 2013 by
Pen & Sword Military
An imprint of
Pen & Sword Books Ltd
47 Church Street
Barnsley
South Yorkshire
S70 2AS

First published in Great Britain in 2011 in digital format by
Coda Books Ltd.

Copyright © Coda Books Ltd, 2011
Published under licence by Pen & Sword Books Ltd.

ISBN 978 1 78159 219 9

A CIP catalogue record for this book is
available from the British Library

All rights reserved. No part of this book may be reproduced or transmitted in any form or by any means, electronic or mechanical including photocopying, recording or by any information storage and retrieval system, without permission from the Publisher in writing.

Printed and bound in Great Britain
by CPI Group (UK) Ltd, Croydon, CR0 4YY

Pen & Sword Books Ltd incorporates the Imprints of Pen & Sword Aviation, Pen & Sword Family History, Pen & Sword Maritime, Pen & Sword Military, Pen & Sword Discovery, Pen & Sword Politics, Pen & Sword Atlas, Pen & Sword Archaeology, Wharncliffe Local History, Wharncliffe True Crime, Wharncliffe Transport, Pen & Sword Select, Pen & Sword Military Classics, Leo Cooper, The Praetorian Press, Claymore Press, Remember When, Seaforth Publishing and Frontline Publishing

For a complete list of Pen & Sword titles please contact
PEN & SWORD BOOKS LIMITED
47 Church Street, Barnsley, South Yorkshire, S70 2AS, England
E-mail: enquiries@pen-and-sword.co.uk
Website: www.pen-and-sword.co.uk

ORIGINAL WARTIME PHOTOGRAPHIC JOURNAL

WAFFEN SS IM WESTEN

(THE WAFFEN SS IN THE WEST)

ORIGINAL 1941 FOREWORD BY GUNTER D'ALQUEN

INTRODUCTION

This photographic journal was originally published in the spring of 1941. It was edited by Hauptsturmführer Gunter d'Alquen, commander of the SS Propaganda Kompanie and editor of the official SS paper, Das Schwarze Korps. D'Alquen also provides the introductory foreword, which launched the exploits of the SS-VT in typical bombastic style.

Gunter d'Alquen was born on 24th October 1910 in Essen; he was the son of a staunchly Protestant businessman who also served as an army reserve officer. D'Alquen attended secondary school in Essen, his generation was the first to grow up under the influence of National Socialism. d'Alquen was a passionate supporter who fully embraced the Nazi political philosophy, he enthusiastically contributed to the movement and joined the Hitler Youth. In 1925 he took up full membership of the NSDAP at the age of just seventeen, he also enrolled in the ranks of the SA and somehow found time to be active as a Party Youth Leader between 1927 and 1931.

As a University student d'Alquen played an active part in the National Socialist German Students' League, but he did not complete his university course and concentrated instead on pursuing a journalistic career. On 10th April 1931 he joined the SS, rising to the rank of SS Hauptsturmführer (Captain) in the relatively short qualifying period of just three years service. In 1932 d'Alquen joined the staff of the Völkischer Beobachter as a political correspondent where he soon came to the attention of Heinrich Himmler. In March 1935, Himmler appointed d'Alquen as editor of the official SS paper, Das Schwarze Korps.

D'Alquen soon became chief spokesman of the SS in the German press and under his editorship the paper fervently trumpeted the National Socialist agenda and relentlessly attacked those who were perceived as enemies of the movement. Intellectuals, greedy capitalists, slackers and communists were all regular targets. The magazine was, of course, also notorious for it's vicious and crude anti-semitism. As the war progressed d'Alquen saw it as his duty to project a positive slant at

The front cover of the original book as first published in 1941.

all times and Das Schwartze Korps regarded itself as a bastion of hope even in the years of defeat and disaster, constantly focussing its attention on German victories at the front however slight these had become.

In January of 1940 an SS-Kriegsberichter-Kompanie (Waffen-SS war reporters company) was established, and its züge (platoons) were attached to the four main Waffen-SS combat formations that fought in the Western Campaign of May and June, 1940. These platoons remained with their respective divisions for the Balkans Campaign in the spring of 1941.

The SS Kriegsberichter Kompanie recorded the actions of the Waffen SS from 1940 onwards.

Gunter d'Alquen commanded the SS-Kriegsberichter unit throughout the war. By 1940 he had attained the Allgemeine-SS rank of Standartenführer, but began his Waffen-SS command in 1940 as a Waffen-SS Hauptsturmführer der Reserve. During the course of the war, he rose through the ranks until he became a Waffen-SS Standartenführer der Reserve and exercised the equivalent of regimental command.

D'Alquen was responsible for a large back room staff, which processed the incoming material, as well as the front line photographers, movie cameramen, writers, broadcaster and recorders, who served in the front lines. The Kreigsberichte in the field were assigned to the various platoons for variable periods of service. Where possible, non-Germans served with their own national formations, but were sometimes detached to cover a particular campaign and report specifically for their own domestic press.

D'Alquen himself was a distinguished SS war reporter and served in the front lines during 1939 and 1940. In 1944 he was appointed by Himmler as head of the entire Wehrmacht propaganda department. Among the books he published was an official history of the SS, "Die SS. Geschichte, Aufgabe und Organisation der Schutzstaffeln der NSDAP" (1939). He also edited "Das ist der Sieg" (1940) and of course the volume originally entitled "Waffen-SS im Westen" (1941), a reprinted version of which you now hold in your hands.

After the war d'Alquen found it difficult to leave his past behind. In July 1955 he was fined DM 60,000 by a Berlin De-Nazification court and deprived of all civic rights for a period of three years and debarred from drawing an allowance or pension from public funds. The court found him guilty of having played an important role in the Third Reich, of war propaganda, incitement against the churches, the Jews and foreign countries, and incitement to murder. He was judged to have glorified the Waffen SS, the Nazi State and reinforced the legend of Hitler's infallibility, he was also adjudged to bring democracy into contempt and encouraged anti-Semitism. After a further investigation into his earnings from Nazi propaganda, d'Alquen was fined another DM 28,000 by the Berlin De-Nazification court on January 7, 1958. He died in 1998.

THE STANDARTE "GERMANIA" AND THE SS VERFÜGUNGS DIVISION (SS-VT)

Many of the pictures taken in this book feature the men of Waffen SS Standarte "Germania". In 1940 the men who bore the word Germania on their cuff bands were fighting as a motorised regiment under the command of SS-Standartenführer Karl-Maria Demelhuber.

Originally Germania was formed in August 1934, as SS-Standarte III. It was soon renamed SS-Standarte II when Hitler ordered that SS-Leibstandarte Adolf Hitler would not be included in the SS numbering sequence. At the 1936 Nürnberg Rally, SS-Standarte II was officially granted the honour title "Germania" where it received the unit colours and authority to wear the cuff band bearing the unit title. It subsequently took a part in the annexation of Austria and was responsible for security during the Italian leader Benito Mussolini's visit to Germany. Germania also took part in the annexation of Sudetenland. It later served as a guard regiment in Prague, as Wach-Regiment des Reichsprotektors von Böhmen und Mähren, until July 1939.

In August 1939 Adolf Hitler, in preparation for Fall Weiss, placed the SS-VT under the operational command of the OKW. At the outbreak of hostilities in Poland, there were four SS armed regiments in existence "Leibstandarte", "Deutschland", "Germania" and the new regiment from Austria named "Der Führer" (although "Der Führer" was not yet combat-ready and played no part in the Polish campaign). Events during the Invasion of Poland raised a political furore with OKW expressing doubts over the combat effectiveness of the SS-VT. Their courage and willingness to fight was never in any doubt; but at times they were almost too eager for action and this naïve enthusiasm led to disproportionately high casualties. The OKW reported that the SS-VT had unnecessarily exposed themselves to risks and acted recklessly, incurring far heavier losses than Army troops and endangering the achievement of operational mission objectives as a result. It was also strongly argued by OKW that the SS-VT was poorly trained and many of its officers were unsuitable for command. In retaliation the SS-VT argued strongly that it had been mishandled and was hampered by it's deployment as sub-units intermixed with regular Wehrmacht forces. Himmler took issue with the fact that SS-VT units were fighting piecemeal with the mixed Wehrmacht/SS Panzer Division Kempf instead of as one SS-VT formation. The SS-VT he argued was also improperly equipped to carry out some of the tasks, which had been allocated of it.

SS-Standartenführer Karl-Maria Demelhuber, Commander of the Germania regiment.

As a result of all this Heinrich Himmler, as always, went too far and insisted that, in future, the SS-VT should be allowed to fight only in the form of it's own discrete formations, under its own commanders and high command. The OKW reacted strongly to this nonsensical suggestion and in response mounted an attempt to have the SS-VT disbanded altogether. Hitler was unwilling to consider this, but neither did he wish to upset the Army and he chose a conciliatory path. Hitler ordered that for the campaign in the West the SS-VT should form its own self contained Division, but this Division and all subsequent Waffen SS divisions would still come under Army command.

Accordingly in October 1939, the "Deutschland", "Germania", "Der Führer" and various support units including artillery and reconnaissance battalions were reorganised into the SS-Verfügungs Division (SS-VT).

Generalleutnant der Waffen-SS Paul "pappa" Hauser.

Initially SS Leibstandarte were earmarked to form part of the formation but the decision was rescinded and SS Leibstandarte did not fight alongside the other units. The SS-Verfügungs Division which took part in Fall Gelb came under the command of Generalleutnant der Waffen-SS Paul "pappa" Hauser and took part in the Campaigns in the West against the Low Countries and France in 1940. This time round the SS-VT distinguished itself in combat and was to win praise from OKW. The SS reconnaissance battalion played a distinguished role in the campaign and many of the photographs in this book feature that formation.

The SS-VT first saw action in the main drive for the Dutch central front and Rotterdam and many of those images are presented in this book. After Rotterdam had been captured, the Division, along with other divisions, intercepted a French force and forced them back to the area of Zeeland and Antwerp. The SS-VT were next used to mop-up small pockets of resistance in the areas already captured by the German advance. The Division was then transferred to France. Despite Hitler's express orders to halt, Sepp Deitrich ordered an advance by his SS Leibstandarte which breached the strongly defended La Bassee canal line, but at a high cost in Waffen SS casualties. Meanwhile the SS-VT division finally participated in the drive on Paris. At the end of the Campaign, it had advanced all the way to the Spanish Frontier.

The SS-Verfügungs Division was later to gain far greater fame when it was re-named as the Waffen SS Division Das Reich. However SS "Germania" had no role to play in that particular formation. The victorious campaign in the West had proved the fighting reputation of the Waffen-SS, and in the process had also opened new and fertile recruiting grounds among the populations of the conquered territories many of whom were sympathetic to the aims of National Socialism. The low countries in particular were to prove a very strong recruiting ground for the Waffen-SS. Initially there were so many volunteers that a new regiment, "Westland", was quickly formed and it's ranks almost immediately filled by Dutch and Belgian volunteers. This was followed by a sister regiment, known as "Nordland", which was formed from the ranks of Norwegian and Danish volunteers.

Soon after the French campaign, "Germania" was detached from the SS-VT division and combined with these two new foreign formations, to form the new 5th SS Division comprised of, "Westland", "Nordland" and "Germania". The division was originally entitled "Germania" but in order to better reflect it's origins it was soon redesignated as the 5th SS Division "Wiking" and was destined to become one of the most controversial fighting formations of the war.

ORIGINAL FOREWORD BY GUNTER D'ALQUEN, COMMANDER OF THE SS-KREIGSBERICHTER KOMPANIE

The fast, unstoppable whirlwind campaign in the west, the march which swept through Holland, Belgium and France has provided us with a new perspective on warfare, it has changed our understanding of war, both from experience at first hand in the field and in the command post. The new tactics developed by the forces of the National Socialist revolution and its new army brought a new mobile dimension to the war, which once again took advantage of the vastness of the great battlefield.

It is the soldier, the individual soldier who is now back in focus after the unimaginative affairs dominated by materiél, which characterised the battles of World War I. The individual soldier is once again the key to the battle, equipped with the best weapons; he buckles his backpack led on by faith, strengthened by the firm and clear conviction that he is the anvil of victory.

In him, in his face, in his attitude during the opening attack, even in exhaustion after yet greater efforts in the long, hot days of incessant combat, can be seen the collective power. He is secure in the strength of this sublime camaraderie; he is focused on the objective oblivious to everything around him. All else is merely background; the vast backdrop of this unfolding drama.

The war reporters of the SS, accompanied the soldiers of our mobile

Gunter d'Alquen, commander of the SS Propaganda Kompanie.

divisions, and took part in the long, hot marches and were present in battles and attacks; their duty was to help preserve the true image of the National Socialist soldiers. They sometimes gave their lives for the cause, they proved that both themselves and the other men of the regiments of the Waffen SS, the infantryman, tank hunter, the artilleryman, will never be equalled.

In the units under my command I know that we have many fine front line photographers who fulfilled their duty. As can be seen from the following pictures, the SS Kriegsberichter Kompanie which was deployed, made a fine contribution to the task of documenting this war. They concentrated from the beginning on the soldier, his face and his attitude in action and was the focal point of this task. These images can never claim to be exhaustive, but they accurately mirror the events of the German war for freedom. The sequence here was taken during the struggles of a division of the Waffen SS in the West; many other parts of the Waffen SS have experienced similar events in the East. This Division, fought and won and the other divisions and regiments of the Waffen SS in future will take strength from that and will ensure that the common desire for victory is fulfilled.

This book and these images will be testimony to the young soldiers of the German army, the proud bearers of the Army's honour, men who gave their best and who lived up to their oath to Adolf Hitler given since the first days of the first Scutszstaffel: "SS man, your honour is loyalty."

Gunter d'Alquen, in the field, February 1941.

Das Gesicht der Waffen SS *(The face of the Waffen-SS)*

"Schnelle Truppen"
("Flying column")

Aufklärungs-sabteilung seit Tagen hinter dem Feind
(A reconnaissance unit behind enemy lines)

The SS Aufklärungsabteilung (Reconnaissance Battalion) was a key component of the SS-VT Division structure. The battalion played a vital part in the French campaign. One of the chief tasks allocated to this fast moving and highly mobile force was to maintain contact with retreating enemy forces.

... *immer im Sattel* | The BMW R75 was the powerful and highly reliable motorcycle, which equipped the Aufklärungsabteilung.
(... constantly in the saddle...)

The addition of the sidecar meant that three men could be transported on each machine, which gave the unit the advantage of mobility with added firepower.

Die Spitzenreiter...
(The leaders...)

Die Lage wird bekanntgegeben
(The objective is about to be announced)

*"**Hier marschiert die Kolonne!**" ("The column will advance to here!")*

Vorwärts auf endloser Straße *(Forward down the endless road)*

Bataillons Gefechtsstand *(Battalion combat status)*

In May 1940 the SS-VT was on alert for the commencement of Fall Gelb (Operation Yellow), which would signal a pre-emptive invasion of the Netherlands and Belgium. The SS Reconnaissance Battalion and The Der Führer Regiment received their movement orders first and on 9th May were detached from the SS-VT Division and moved near the Dutch border, with the remainder of the division remaining behind the lines in Munster.

Frühmorgens, eh die Hähne krähn
(Early in the morning, before the cock crows)

In die Bereitstellung
(In the assembly area)

Holland... Elements of The SS-VT Division first saw action in Holland at 5:35 am on 10th May 1940 when "Der Führer" and the SS Aufklärungsabteilung captured Arnhem and advanced towards Utrecht. The reconnaissance battalion had been split into five groups consisting of a motorcycle platoon and two armoured cars each and tasked with the objective of capturing an intact bridge over the Maas-Waal canal.

Assault Teams One and Three failed to achieve their objectives and Team One sustained heavy casualties after the bridge at Neerbosch was blown by retreating Dutch forces. However assault teams Two and Four succeeded in securing crossing points at Hatert and Heumen respectively.

...auf schmalen Dämmen durch überschwemmtes Land
(...A flat waterlogged country protected by dams)

Kurz vor der Feindberührung *(Shortly before enemy contact)*

The following day, the remainder of the SS-VT Division in three March columns crossed into Holland ordered to penetrate the Grebbe defence line then spearhead the thrust towards Rotterdam. Dutch resistance was expected to be protracted making the assault a costly prospect, however "Der Führer" regiment attacked the heavily defended Grebbe mountain position after a heavy artillery bombardment and captured their objective by 1900 hrs on 12th May 1940.

Noch ist die Gruppe geschlossen *(The group maintains close order)*

Munitionsschütze
(Ammunition carrier)

Schütze 3 *(Trooper number 3)*

Das schwere MG
(The heavy machine gun)

In the first campaign of the war the SS-VT was equipped with the highly effective MG 34. It could be operated as a light machine gun using its integral bipod stand, which was mounted underneath the barrel, or turned into a heavy machine gun by the simple expedient of mounting the gun on a tripod. However the MG 34 in combat conditions proved to be somewhat over engineered which rendered the MG34 vulnerable to stoppage at crucial moments. The practical rate of fire in Light Machine gun mode was around 100-200 rounds per minute. Tripod mounted in heavy machine gun mode the effective rate of fire was 300 rounds per minute. The effective range in light machine gun mode was 600-800 yards, rising to 2000-2500 yards in heavy machine gun mode.

Gegenüber der Feind *(Observing the enemy)*

Jetzt ist die Luftwaffe dran (Now the air force arrives)

Der Divisions Kommandeur
(The divisional ommander - Paul Hausser)

Das war ein Tag!
(That was someday!)

The fighting in Holland is often viewed as being one sided and half hearted from the point of view of the Dutch forces. However the "Der Führer" regiment in particular suffered very heavy casualties in the first few days amounting to over four hundred with one hundred and twenty killed and two hundred and fifty wounded by 12th May.

Im Sprung über den Damm
(The fast rush over the lane)

Der Wald ist gesäubert
(The forest is cleared)

For the Holland campaign, The SS Leibstandarte had been incorporated into the Army's 27th Infantry Division and on 10th May spearheaded the northern flank German advance into Holland. The SS Totenkopf and SS Polizei Divisions were held in reserve. After the surrender of Rotterdam, the Leibstandarte set out to capture The Hague, which they achieved on 15th May, capturing 3,500 Dutch prisoners of war.

Das Schützenloch
(The foxhole)

Ich hatt...
(I had...)

The original caption on these two pages were taken from the first line of the famous German military lament "Ich hatt' einen Kameraden". The text was written by the German poet Ludwig Uhland in 1809, but it was not until 1822 that the composer Friedrich Silcher set it to music. This piece would have been instantly recognisable to contemporary audiences and is still used at military funerals today.

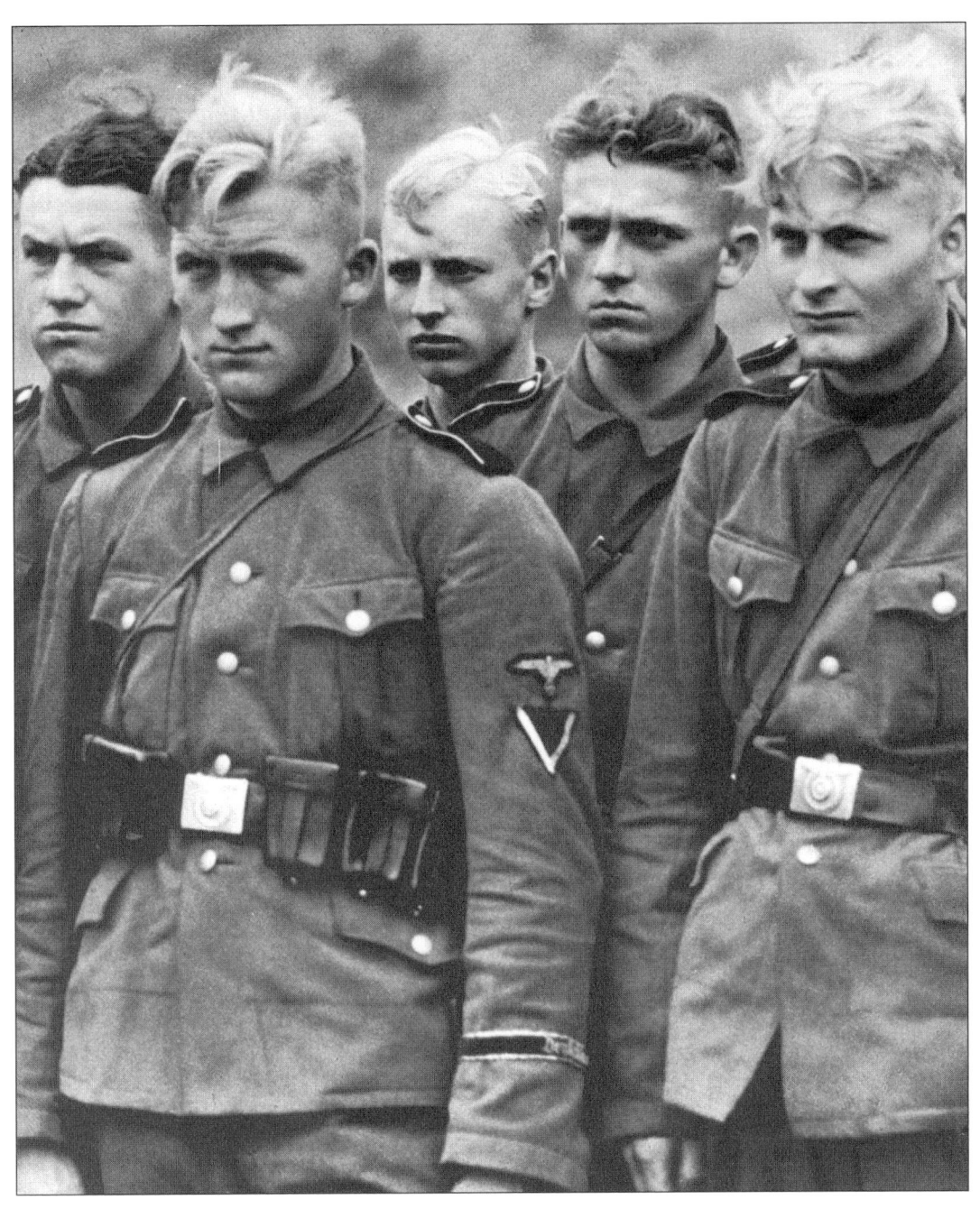

... Einen Kameraden (... A comrade)

Nach schnellem Stoß das letzte Haus erreicht *(After a quick halt the last house is reached)*

Fighting in an urban landscape was particularly stressful and costly. The buildings damaged or otherwise afforded the defender the advantage. With the upper storeys of buildings available to snipers and machine gunners the attacking Waffen SS had to think in three-dimensions and consequently expend greater amounts of ammunition and manpower in urban battles.

Die Spitze *(The conclusion)*

Unser Jüngster
(Our youngster)

The tactical unit of the Waffen SS was the ten-man squad, which comprised a squad leader and his deputy, a four-man rifle group and a machine gun group. The four-man machine gun group operated two MG34s and provided the bulk of the squad's firepower both in offence and defence. The squad generally employed the machine gun elements to provide suppressive fire while the rifle element advanced to neutralise the enemy with grenades and rifle fire. The most common role of the rifle group was therefore to support and protect the machine gun group. The rifle element also functioned as an assault group on the attack where they were charged with taking and holding ground.

Auf der Lauer
(On the lookout)

Das Dorf wird durchgekämmt
(The village is captured)

On 14th May the SS-VT division found itself pitched against French forces for the first time. French armoured forces had entered Holland in support of the Dutch. The Panzerjager detachment of SS Deutschsland soon distinguished itself knocking out five Renault tanks and a number of armoured cars.

Dutch resistance lasted until 15th May but French forces and English forces continued to resist the German forces in Holland and Northern Belgium. The SS-VT was involved in heavy fighting against French forces around Achterbroek. Fighting continued on Walcheren Island until 18th May.

Straße unter Feuer
(Road under fire)

Pak ist vorne
(Anti-tank gun to the front)

On 21st May elements of the SS-VT division were involved in the Battle Of Arras against the British 5th division, which attacked the German invaders with a strong force including around seventy tanks. It was a close run thing and the SS-VT division suffered twenty dead and thirty wounded in the course of the morning.

Der Zugführer (The Squad Leader)

Und jetzt – der Sprung!
(And now – the rush!)

Kurz Atem holen
(A quick rest)

Pak ohne Motor *(Anti-tank gun on the move)*

On 24th May British forces attacked Saint Venant, forcing the SS-VT Division to retreat. This was a significant event as it marked the first time any SS unit had been forced to withdraw and surrender ground that it had captured to the enemy. However the advance was soon resumed and on 27th May "Deutschland" reached a river line at Merville.

... aber mit Männern...
(... with the crew...)

... anpacken...
(... ready...)

On 27th May elements of the SS-VT formed a bridgehead across the river and waited for the detached Panzerjager plaatoon SS Totenkopf Division to arrive and provide support and cover their exposed flank. However, the men of the "Deutschland" regiment were surprised by a unit of British tanks unexpectedly advanced on their positions. The SS-VT just managed to hold out against the British tank force, which penetrated to within fifteen feet of German positions. The day was rescued by the arrival of the Totenkopf Panzerjager platoon, which saved the "Deutschland" from what seemed like certain destruction.

... richten...
(... aim...)

... feuern...
(... fire...)

... und treffen...
(... and a hit.)

Gefährliches Handwerk
(Dangerous handiwork)

Der Sieger *(The victor)*

Das hat gesessen! *(Under counter attack!)*

Auf, marsch, marsch! *(Onwards, advance, advance!)*

Infanterie... Infanterie! *(Infantry... infantry!)*

Heiße Tage... *(Hot days...)*

... heiße Nächte (... Hot nights)

Das war in Aire
(The war in Aire)

Das war in Aire

On the night of May 23rd the SS-VT had to contend with a strong breakthrough by a large French force supported by tanks. In a fierce night battle three French tanks were knocked out in the streets of the town by members of the "Germania" motorcycle infantry company.

Die motorisierte Deckung (*The motor provides cover*)

Mit und...
(with and...)

During the closing battles with the British expeditionary force, the SS-VT enjoyed the welcome support of the 8th Panzer Division which fought on the left flank of SS "Der Fürher" and was much needed given the large armoured contingents available to the French and British forces.

... hinter dem Panzer *(... behind the tank)*

Weiter, immer weiter (The advance continues more and more)

Der Kompanietrupp *(The company group)*

Achtung, was... *(Attention, what's...)*

The British Armour continued to pose problems for the Germans who needed to allow the heavier British tanks to close to suicidally short distances in order for the puny 37mm PAK to penetrate the frontal armour of the British armoured vehicles.

gibt's da vorn?
(... up ahead?)

Die Fahrzeuge sind zurückgeblieben
(The vehicles are left behind)

After the Dutch surrender, the Leibstandarte moved south to France on 24th May where they became part of the XIX Panzer Corps under the command of General Heinz Guderian. The Leibstandarte took up a position fifteen miles south west of Dunkirk along the line of the Aa canal, with a bridgehead established at Saint Venant. That night the OKW issued an order that the advance was to be halted despite the fact that the British Expeditionary Force was obviously trapped.

Der Stoßtrupp
(Shock troops)

Nur keinen Laut!
(No sound)

**Befehl ausgeführt.
– Sammeln!**
(Orders – gather round!)

The Leibstandarte paused for the night of the 24th May as ordered. On the following day however, in defiance of Hitler's orders, the Leibstandarte continued the advance. Dietrich ordered the LAH's third battalion to cross the canal and capture the heights beyond, where British artillery observers were directing highly accurate artillery fire, which was causing heavy casualties. The third battalion assaulted the heights and overran the British positions. After the fall of France, despite his act of insubordination, Sepp Dietrich was awarded the Knight's Cross of the Iron Cross by a delighted Adolf Hitler.

***Führer,
Unterführer
und Mann***
*(Leader, Sub-Officer
and men)*

The 27th of May was a black day in the history of the Waffen SS when a unit from the Totenkopf (the 14th Company) was involved in the Le Paradis massacre, in which ninety-nine unarmed men of the 2nd Battalion, Royal Norfolk Regiment were machine gunned, the survivors were killed with bayonets.

Auf dem Anstand *(On the look out)*

Wann geht's los? *(When's it happening?)*

Vor einer großen Sache *(Before a big event)*

Ort und...
(Objective reached and...)

The SS-VT Division was engaged against the cream of the British Expeditionary Force, which included strong armoured contingents and inevitably resulted in high German casualties.

By 28th May the Leibstandarte had taken Wormhout only ten miles from Dunkirk. Unfortunately the reputation of the Waffen SS was stained by a further atrocity which occurred here and has become known to an unforgiving posterity as the Wormhoudt massacre when the second battalion of the Leibstandarte killed eighty British prisoners of war in cold blood.

... Gelände sind zu säubern!
(... Grounds are clear!)

Aus der Deckung
(From the cover)

Between the 27th and 29th May the SS-VT were engaged in the fierce battles to dislodge the British forces from the Nieppe forest where the terrain was highly favourable to the defenders. German casualties were again high.

Der Chef weist ein *(The commander issues orders)*

Der Spähtruppführer
(Advance troop leader)

Elements of the SS V-T were also engaged in attacking the remaining French forces in the battles for Hazerouk, Cassel, Baliieul and Poperinghe, which raged from 27th to 31st May.

Bataillonsadjutant verwundet
(The battalion adjutant is wounded)

Pünktlich wie immer, unsere Stukas
(Our Stukas are punctual as always)

Dive bomber support was a key element in the early campaigns of the war. In France the Luftwaffe was still in a position to operate with relative impunity and provided timely interventions at vital moments.

Meter um Meter...
(Metre by metre...)

... kriecht die Kompanie...
(... crawls the company...)

Following the battles of Artois and Flanders, which saw collapse of the Belgians and the withdrawal of the British, the new operation to destroy all remaining allied forces in France was launched; it was codenamed Fall Rot (Operation Red).

... in Erwartung des entscheidenden Augenblicks
(...in anticipation of the decisive moment)

Kurze Rast
(A short break)

By the 4th June 1940 the bulk of the British Expeditionary Force had been forced to withdraw from Dunkirk. However, even with the British now out of the picture, there was nonetheless still plenty of hard fighting to come against the remaining French armies which were still intact and determined to defend their homeland.

Das Feuer wird vorverlegt *(Forward towards the fire)*

*"**Angriffsziel erreicht!**" ("The target for the attack!")*

Jetzt hat die Artillerie das Wort
(Now, the artillery)

Der Frontsoldat von 1940 *(The frontline soldier of 1940)*

Schlaf ist wichtig...
(Sleep is vital...)

On 1st June 1940 the SS-VT Division was attached to Group Von Kleist and enjoyed a brief period for rest and regrouping. It is a sobering indication of just how tough the fighting had been that the SS-VT Division which had been in action for a little less than three weeks required 2020 replacements who were fed in to the division from replacement units and incorporated into the ranks ready for the next stage of the fight.

... wie Munition (... with the ammunition)

Gut getarnt ist halb gewonnen
(Good camouflage is half the battle)

On June 4th the first SS-VT forces were committed to the Fall Rot operation which began with an artillery duel near Peronne and cost the SS Artillery regiment two killed and seventeen wounded.

Gleich geht's weiter *(Just go on)*

Und dann die Pioniere (Here come the pioneers)

On 6th June the advanced guard of "Germania" were involved in fighting on the old first world war battlefields of The Somme. The troopers observed that many trenches were still recognisable.

"Über die Schelde, die Maas und den Rhein..."
("Over the Schelde, The Maas or the Rhine...)

Wasser ist...
(Water is...)

The Division continued to drive south and on 7th June "Der Führer" made the first contact with French forces at Roye when the SS Aufklärungsabteilung captured two retreating field guns and two hundred French prisoners.

*... **kein Aufenthalt** (... no deterrent)*

Am anderen Ufer *(On the other side)*

Advance elements of "Der Führer" met an Alerian force in company strength, which was almost entirely wiped out in a fierce firefight, which took place just outside Bouchoir.

Schnell die Brücke her! *(Quick, the obstacle!)*

Der Beobachter *(The lookout)*

Bouchoir was turned into a strong point for French resistance. The retreating French forces army managed to briefly re-establish some equilibrium and mounted a surprisingly strong defence which took the SS-VT by surprise and resulted in unexpectedly heavy casualties.

Der Feuerschutz
(Covering fire)

Rottenführer und Mann *(Section leader and trooper)*

"In confronting the Belgian-Franco-British army's attempts to break out of it's encirclement, which drew the bulk of the division into the Nieppe Forest, we demonstrated our superiority even against the stubbornly combative British forces. The battle of the Nieppe forest against an unyielding defence supported by tanks, is now a page of honour in the young history of the Regiments "Der Führer", "Germania" and the Waffen SS Reconnaissance Battalion."

Hausser
SS Gruppenführer
Division Order of the day 3rd June 1940

Über das freie Feld
(In the open field)

Kampfpause
(A lull in the fighting)

The French air force remained surprisingly active well into the campaign and on the night of 8th June the advance elements of SS-VT in the Weygand line were subjected to extensive night bombing near Montdidier.

Der Unterscharführer
(The junior squad leader)

Ist ja halb so schlimm!
(It's not half as bad!)

On 7th June nine armoured cars of the Aufklärungsabteilung advancing from Bouchoir were involved in heavy fighting outside Le Quesnel with well dug in French forces equipped with armour piercing weapons. One eight wheel armoured car was lost and its crew wounded before the force could withdraw. The other vehicles all suffered significant battle damage.

Der Arzt bringt sie zurück
(Brought back to the doctor)

Nochmal gut gegangen *(Once again, all is well)*

Jeder wird gefunden
(Everyone will receive aid)

Abgesessen
(Dismounted)

Wo bleibt der Tommy?
(Where is Tommy?)

Ein schneller Schluck *(A quick drink)*

Die Artillerie des kleinen Mannes
(Artillery for the little man)

At dusk on 8th June the "Der Führer" Regiment was strongly assaulted by a regiment of the French Foreign Legion, which was found to comprise both French and German units. The attack was broken up by artillery fire from the SS Artillery Regiment.

Der lange Arm der Infanterie
(The long arm of the infantry)

On 8th June a fierce artillery duel took place between the SS Artillery regiment and a French battery stationed around Marquevilliers, which resulted in the destruction of the French battery.

Abgefeuert! *(Fire!)*

Nichts wie runter von den Krädern!
(Nothing like the motorbike!)

On 12th June Kleist's Panzer group received reinforcement in the form of the SS "Liebstandarte" and also the remaining elements of the SS "Totenkopf" Division which had been held in reserve. All three Waffen SS formations fighting in France were now to be found in the same formation.

Pak wird vorgezogen *(Anti-tank guns are preferred)*

Hundert Meter Straßengraben...
(One hundred metres along the road ditch)

... sind eine Meile weit *(... and another bound)*

Vorwärts, Vorwärts *(Forward, forward)*

On 9th June the SS-VT division was involved in heavy fighting on the banks of the river Avre which required additional support from the Stukas of the Luftwaffe to break French resistance. The Division suffered 24 killed and 113 wounded between 6th and 9th June.

Doch der Segen kommt von oben
(But the blessings come from above)

Wie tausendmal geübt
(As practiced a thousand times)

Ich hatt' einen Kameraden

Ich hatt' einen Kameraden, …*I had a comrade,*
Einen bessern findst du nit, …*You'll never find a better one,*
Die Trommel schlug zum Streite, …*The drum called us to battle,*
Er ging an meiner Seite, …*He was always by my side,*
In gleichem Schritt und Tritt. …*In step, with measured stride.*

Eine Kugel kam geflogen, …A bullet flew towards us,
Gilt's mir oder gilt es dir? …For him or meant for me?
Ihn hat es weggerissen, …His life from mine it tore,
Er liegt vor meinen Füßen, …Wounded he lay at my feet,
Als wär's ein Stück von mir. …I felt I'd lost a part of me.

Will mir die Hand noch reichen, …His hand reached up to hold mine,
Derweil ich eben lad, …But I must load my gun,
Kann dir die Hand nicht geben, …I cannot give you my hand now,
Bleib du im ew'gen Leben, …In life eternal we'll meet again,
Mein guter Kamerad! …My good comrade!

Doch mancher bleibt zurück
(But some were left behind)

Achtung, hier stinkt's *(Attention, here we)*

The crumbling French forces were to be allowed no time to rest and regroup. A new directive issued on 14th June by Hitler stressed the need for "sharp pursuit" of the French in order to prevent the possibility of their forming a new front south of Paris.

Verfolgung
(Follow)

Widerstand im Ort... *(Resistance in the city...)*

On 17th June the SS-VT Division found itself involved in aggressive combat operations centred on Troyes as the three regiments of the SS-VT Division made a successful attempt to disrupt and capture retreating French forces.

... ist bald gebrochen
(... will soon be broken)

Der Kradmelder
(The motorcycle despatch rider)

The last heavy resistance encountered by SS-VT troops took place on 17th June in the heavily forested area north of Carillon where the fighting was centred on the village of Molsemes. From that point onwards, although there were still a number of combat actions, the SS-VT division was essentially involved in seizing ground and mopping up prisoners.

"Hau ab!" *("Away you go!")*

Zwischen zwei Aufträgen *(Between two despatches)*

Between 19th and 25th June a series of rapid advances by elements of the SS-VT led by the SS Aufklärangsabteilung succeeded in capturing large numbers of the French forces retreating to the southeast.

Dafür gab's nur wenig Zeit (But there's not much time)

Soldat und Berichter... *(Soldier and reporter...)*

... *Kriegsberichter* (... War reporter)

Anschluß, Anschluß!
(The link up!)

On 22nd June the last combat effective French army still in the field was encircled and 500,000 men marched into captivity. The campaign in France was effectively over.

Gleich muß der Melder kommen *(Waiting for the orders to come)*

Nur ein paar Zeilen *(Only time for a few lines)*

Für Pflichterfüllung (Awards for dedication to duty)

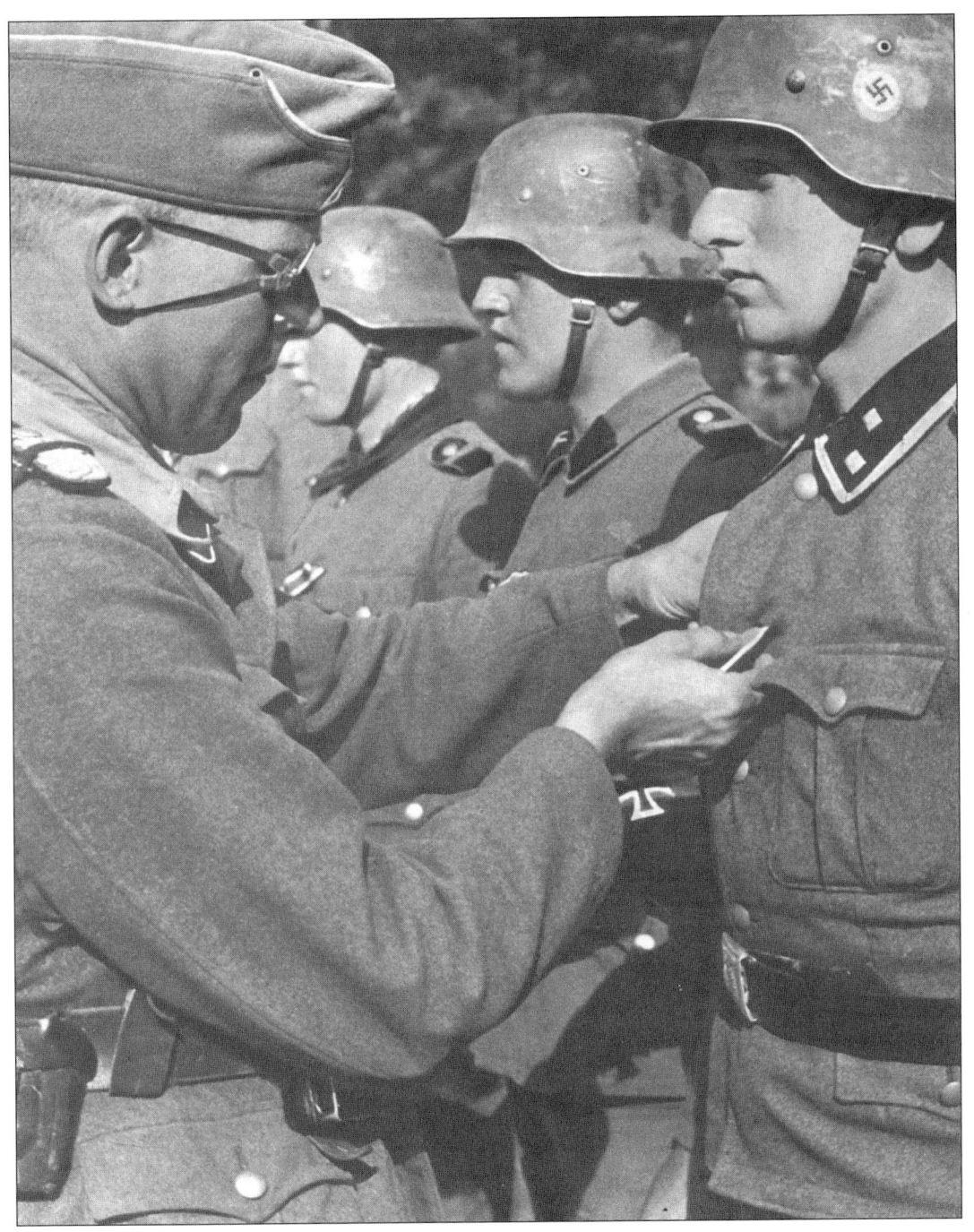

"... marschieren wir, marschieren wir nach Frankreich hinein!"

("... we march, we march into France!")

The order to cease-fire came at 01:35 hours on 25th June 1940. The battle for France was finally over. For the SS-VT there was still work to do as the battalion was tasked with occupying southwest France to the Spanish border.

More from the same series

Most books from the 'Hitler's War Machine' series are edited and endorsed by Emmy Award winning film maker and military historian Bob Carruthers, producer of Discovery Channel's Line of Fire and Weapons of War and BBC's Both Sides of the Line. Long experience and strong editorial control gives the military history enthusiast the ability to buy with confidence.

Tiger I in Combat

Tiger I Crew Manual

Panzers at War 1939-1942

Panzers at War 1943-1945

Wolf Pack - the U boats

Poland 1939

Luftwaffe Combat Reports

Sturmgeschütze

German Artillery in Combat

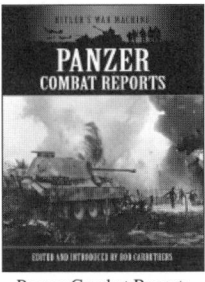
Panzer Combat Reports

The Panther V in Combat

German Tank Hunters

The Afrika Korps in Combat

Panzers I & II

Panzer III

Panzer IV

For more information visit www.pen-and-sword.co.uk